Green Tea

Green Tea

The Delicious Everyday
Health Drink

Peter Oppliger

Saffron Walden
The C.W. Daniel Company Ltd

First published in Switzerland in 1996
by Midena Verlag, Küttigen

This English-language edition first published in Great Britain in 1998
by The C. W. Daniel Company Limited
1 Church Path, Saffron Walden,
Essex, CB10 1JP, United Kingdom

Photographs: Evelyn and Hans-Peter König, Zurich, and the author

ISBN 0 85207 321 6

Designed by Jim Reader.
Designed and produced in association with
Book Production Consultants plc, Cambridge, England.
Typeset by Cambridge Photosetting Services, Cambridge, England.
Printed and bound in Singapore by Kyodo Printing Co (S'pore) Pte Ltd.

Contents

The Tea Plant

Historically, culturally and therapeutically, the tea plant is one of the most fascinating of all medicinal herbs. It is widely consumed in the form of black tea and green tea.

After water, tea is the most popular beverage consumed anywhere in the world and is mainly known as 'black tea' and 'green tea'. Even the Eskimos are great tea-drinkers! In many countries, tea-drinking is part of the culture; in Zen Buddhism, it is part of the religious ceremony and, particularly in Britain and Commonwealth countries, life without tea traditions such as early morning tea, afternoon tea or high tea would be unthinkable. Nevertheless, many people know very little about tea and the highly interesting tea plant.

The aim of this book is to give an informative insight into the secrets of tea. As a specialist in naturopathy, my main intention is to pay tribute to the original art of tea-drinking. By that I mean *green* tea, as a meaningful remedy and a source of enjoyment.

The history of tea, the most important terms from the fascinating world of tea, as well as some scientific explanations and comparisons, will give the reader a better understanding of the special aspects of green tea in comparison with black tea.

No other beverage can combine and complement the properties of a remedy and enjoyment so perfectly. No other beverage has such a traditional history, going back over thousands of years, as green tea.

I think it is important to point out that the Australian tea tree (*Melaleuca alternifolia* from the *Myrtaceae* family) which has become popular in aromatherapy as a source of tea-tree oil should not be confused with the tea plant or tea tree or tea bush *(Camellia sinensis)*! They are completely different plants.

The tea plant 'Camellia sinensis', formerly called 'Thea sinensis'.
The illustration (copperplate print) comes from the "Handbook of
all medical-pharmaceutical herbs" ("Hand-Atlas sämmtlicher
medicinisch-pharmaceutischer Gewächse"), dating from 1857 and
compiled by an "Association of Scholars".

General Information on Tea Cultivation

The tea plant *Camellia sinensis* and the larger species *Camellia assamica*, together with the species *C. viridis, japonica, saranqua*, etc. which have been cultivated or assimilated from them, are the parent strains of the tea plant (leaf). The tea leaves are picked in the sub-tropical areas of cultivation in Darjeeling, Japan and Ceylon etc. from spring through to autumn and, in tropical upland plantations, e.g. in Malaysia, even throughout the entire year.

In the 18th century, Carl von Linné, the renowned Swedish botanist and doctor, and his team studied most of the world's plants and categorized them into the system of plant families which is still valid today. In the course of this work he also included the tea plant, but only as a parent strain, calling it *Thea sinensis L.* Subsequent botanists noted that the plant had assimilated itself to new locations and developed differently. They gave the *Thea sinensis* of the *Camellia* or *Theaceae* family a new name – *Camellia sinensis* – and designated the further types of tea plant according to their locations.

The two parent strains of tea are evergreen trees originating in Asia (in the areas of Darjeeling, Assam and China). In its original locations, *Camellia sinensis* grows to a height of four to six metres, *Camellia assamica* up to nine metres and even up to twelve and more metres under ideal conditions. According to some botanists, *C. assamica* is a wild version of *C. sinensis*.

The tea plant is an evergreen shrub or tree. The alternately arranged leaves are longitudinally ovate, have pointed tips and are finely serrated. The blossom is white and has five petals with a pleasant fragrance. The fruit is triangular in shape and somewhat woody. The tea plant needs a tropical or sub-tropical rainforest climate and thrives at altitudes of 2,100 metres above sea-level. The higher the region, the smaller the tea bush and, consequently, the smaller the crop.

In the typical upland regions such as Darjeeling and Assam as well as in sub-tropical plantation areas, plucking is limited to the summer season. In a

few tropical areas at altitudes of around 1,000 metres, such as in Malaysia, harvesting is a year-round occupation.

In order to facilitate harvesting, the trees are cultivated as shrubs. Depending on location and method of cultivation, it is therefore equally correct to talk of a tea tree, tea shrub or tea bush. Most tea specialists give preference to *Camellia sinensis*. Green tea comes almost exclusively from this species or from *C. japonica* in Japan.

Nowadays, two methods of tea cultivation are prevalent. According to the traditional method, the seeds are sprouted under damp burlap before being planted out in seed beds or plastic pots. However, the more common method of propagation is vegetative, by means of cuttings grown in greenhouses or under plastic roofs.

In traditional tea-growing areas, leaves in various stages of growth are harvested weekly by hand, mostly by women pluckers. The general rule in manual-plucking is that the new shoots are harvested in the form of two leaves and one bud. In many of the newer 'tea-gardens' (tea plantations) of modern countries, such as in Malaysia, machines are used for harvesting. Naturally, only the time-consuming hand-plucking method permits the usual and traditional quality sorting of the harvest into older and younger leaves or even just young shoots, which are then subdivided into many sorting grades.

On some tea plantations in Japan, a combination of manual and machine plucking is used, with the first harvest of spring (first flush) being picked manually as a select, very high quality tea, with subsequent harvests being plucked by machine.

Skilled pluckers harvest 30–35 kg of fresh tea per day. This produces 7–9 kg of dried, ready-to-use tea.

ABOVE: *Traditional hand-pluckers in Japan*

DOUBLE-SPREAD ON THE PRECEDING PAGES: *Tea plantation in the Japanese Shizuoka district. The tea plant, which originally grows as a tree, is cultivated as a bush on the plantations.*

Tea throughout History

The earliest Chinese writings reveal that tea was already in use as a remedy as far back as the year 2700 B.C.

Every story that lasts through the centuries is based on legends, and this is also the case with tea.

The oldest Chinese tea legend relates how, in the year 2737 B.C., the emperor of the time, Shen Nung, learnt of the medicinal properties of tea when a tea leaf dropped from a tree into a pot of boiling water beneath.

A Buddhist legend tells of a Bodhi-Dharma (monk), whose eyes kept closing while he was meditating. As a penance for his tiredness, he cut off his eyelids and threw them to the ground. These sent down roots into the earth and, as a symbol of eternal vigilance, the shoots grew into the first tea shrub.

It is no coincidence that the central figure in the second legend is a Buddhist monk, since it was primarily monks who cultivated tea in their monastery gardens and spread their tea culture throughout China, Tibet and parts of India, as well as in Japan.

From legend to reality

We are all eager to know how mankind ever gained the knowledge in those ancient times that a root, a leaf or a blossom could be used for healing a particular organ in the human body. It is most certainly false to assume that people in earlier times simply acquired this knowledge by experimentation: giving sick people infusions, decoctions of plant extracts, frequently even from highly poisonous plants, and then, dependent on the result, coming to the conclusion that a plant was poisonous if a person died or that the plant had medicinal properties if a person was cured. Probably the only explanation that sheds any light on the matter is that people today have lost their powers of intuition or their 'feel' in favour of rationality. When we observe non-domesticated animals living in the wild, it is clear that these animals can always differentiate between plants for food, plants to cure and poisonous plants in their native vegetation. We can therefore assume that the animals' intuition is still functioning perfectly. This undoubtedly applied to primitive man and people of former generations: they were much closer to nature and could intuitively differentiate between food plants, medicinal plants and poisonous ones.

The history of tea starts in China

Tea – or Ch'a – undoubtedly has its origins in China. It is documented that, under the first Han emperors (202 B.C. – 1 A.D.), tea plants were cultivated independently by the monasteries in Sichuan. However, it was not until the 6th century that tea became the popular drink for all levels of society in China and Tibet. Soon afterwards, the garden-style cultivation of tea spread to parts of India and to Japan, in particular. Tea was not just a popular drink but was always also an important part of Zen Buddhism ceremonies and, in addition, was highly esteemed as a medicine.

The Ch'a Ching, a book dedicated to tea, was produced around the year 800 A.D. The author was Lu Yu, an orphan who had been raised in a Buddhist monastery by monks and was trained as a medicinal herb specialist.

Tea in Japan

There is no doubt that small quantities of tea had already been brought to Japan around the 6th century A.D. by Buddhist monks from China. As a result of the establishment of Buddhism in Japan, tea-drinking also spread. In the 12th century, tea plants were imported on a large scale from China and planted in Japan. The tea plant *Camellia sinensis* apparently acclimatized particularly well in Japan, with the result that botanists spoke of *Camellia japonica*.

Japanese tea culture has developed independently, both in the Zen ceremonies and secular Japanese society. Health awareness is still associated with tea-drinking in Japan today.

Japan's tea tradition has been fully retained in the production of a wide variety of green tea qualities (q.v. chapter 'Green Tea', page 43). In Japan, only green tea is produced.

Tea finds its way to Europe

In the 14th century, the first news of this strange drink reached Europe via the Silk Road.

The first European to be seriously interested in tea after first-hand experience of it in China was the Portuguese Jesuit priest, Jasper de Cruz, in 1560. With their highly modern fleet of ships at that time, the Portuguese also claimed the first trading rights between China and Europe. Thus the first tea to come as merchandise arrived in Lisbon. Dutch ships took the tea on to France, Holland and the Baltic countries. In 1602, the alliance between the Portuguese and the Dutch thrones came to an end, with the result that Holland assumed sole rights for the tea trade.

Tea in Russia

In 1618, the Chinese ambassador to Moscow presented Czar Alexis with several chests of tea. This resulted in a flourishing tea trade from China to Russia. History books give accounts of 200–300 camels constantly plying as tea caravans between China and Moscow during the summer months. The Russian people were particularly appreciative of tea as a hot, energy-giving drink in the winter. The samovar, a combination of water boiler and tea jug, developed according to a Tibetan model, was soon found in every Russian household.

Tea reaches America

In 1650, Peter Stuyvesant, the famous Governor General of New Netherland in America, had tea sent to the Dutch settlers in New Amsterdam, which later became New York. Heavily taxed, this tea soon found its way to the British settlers in the sparsely populated continent of North America, particularly to Boston.

British tea history

The first supplies of tea reached Britain in the years 1652 to 1654. Like tropical spices, tea, which was initially a highly expensive merchandise, was an exclusive product affordable only by the aristocracy and rich merchants. When Britain became involved in the tea trade, the volume of trade that reached Europe and America also increased correspondingly in the competition between the various fleets. Tea gradually became accessible to the middle-class population. Thus Britain experienced a more intense 'tea frenzy' than any of the other countries.

In Britain, as well as in France and Holland, many tea houses and even tea gardens sprang up alongside the existing coffee houses. These provided musical entertainment as well as the highest level of tea culture. Around 1800, there were over 500 tea houses and coffee houses in London alone.

The tradition of 'tea gardens' and 'tea rooms' still exists throughout Britain. Many now lack the musical entertainment and the quality of tea is unfortunately reduced, with few exceptions, to teabag level. The original, famed British tea culture has been maintained until the present day in India, Australia and New Zealand with greater adherence to its pure form than in Britain.

Since coffee had arrived in Europe before tea, coffee houses remained in existence, but served increasing quantities of tea. This change is quite understandable nowadays with people's increasing awareness of health, and may be one that will remain not just wishful thinking on the part of the author.

Tea colonialism

From the mid-19th century, the British started cultivating tea on plantations in their colonies of India and Ceylon (Sri Lanka). Previously, China and Japan had been the largest producers of tea. This was always green tea, the dried and unfermented leaves of the tea plant. In Japan today, only green tea is produced.

It was only at the start of the 20th century that black tea made its appearance with its 'new' flavours. The production of black tea

THE
REGENCY RESTAURANT
& TEA ROOMS
Fully Licensed

was increasingly perfected in British tea plantations. This new British tea culture quickly spread throughout Europe. Production was increased and tea was brought in the famous tea clippers of the British merchant navy in contests around Cape Horn. The fastest ships always did the best business with the new harvest.

In Ceylon the former coffee plantations where the trees had succumbed to disease were burned down in 1870 and replaced with tea plants. In addition, large sections of jungle in the mountains were cleared and further plantations developed. Since the Singhalese farmers were not interested in giving up their small farms to go and work for the British as plantation workers, the English brought Tamils from southern India as a workforce to Ceylon, where they have never really settled to this day.

At the end of the last and the beginning of this century, tea cultivation areas extended to parts of Indonesia, Russia, Asia Minor, Africa and even to South America. Global tea production currently amounts to between 2 and 2.5 million tons annually.

The tea trade today

Tea wholesaling today is mostly in the hands of brokers, as they are known, who sell tea at auctions in the major commercial centres of Calcutta and Colombo to buyers from all parts of the world. These brokers, whose quality-awareness is acute, buy their merchandise, whenever possible, directly from the producers they know.

Tea substitutes

In the early days of tea history in China, this precious 'drug' was not available everywhere and was very expensive. We know from history that the leaves of wild apples, pears and even the wild tea-rose were often used as substitutes for real green tea.

During the two World Wars, tea, as well as coffee, was rare in Europe. Just like the substitute coffee products, there were substitutes for tea. For example, there was a market in Europe for 'Swiss tea', the leaves of the mountain avens *(Dryas octopetala)*, a beautiful Alpine plant.

Mate tea *(Ilex paraguariensis*, q.v. mate tea, page 28), highly popular among the Indians of South America even today, is still wrongly known as 'green tea' by many dealers.

The Name 'Tea'

The original Asian names for tea are very similar to each other: in China it is 'ch'a', in India 'tschaj', in Japan 'cha' and in Russia 'caj'; in English 'tea' and in German 'Tee'.

There could be some relation between the original word 'chi' for vitality (today also used for light power or biophoton energy) and the word 'ch'a'.

In the early stages of European tea history, the tea drink was also called 'cha' in England, Holland and Portugal. At the end of the 17th century 'cha' became 'tay', and a little later 'Tee' and 'tea'.

With tea imports from Asia to Europe, the name 'tea' was also used for our herbal infusions. In our linguistic area, the herbal infusions took on the general designation 'herbal teas'.

The cultures of Asia, particularly those of China, India, Tibet and Japan, were mainly familiar with the tea-leaf infusions, first as a remedy and then as a popular drink. Numerous other medicinal plants were used mostly in the form of powders, pastes and herbal pills; or they were smoked or took other forms. The tea brick, as it is known, contains aspects of traditional medicinal plant preparation (q.v. the chapter 'A Dictionary of Tea').

*In China and Tibet, 'tea bricks' are the traditional way of storing
and trading tea in the form of decorative panels.*

Qualities and Grades
(Sorting Grades)

The quality of a tea is dependent on:

- its *origins* (soil properties, altitude, climate)
- the *care* given to the tea plants (cutting back, spraying with pesticides and insecticides, fertilizer or biological cultivation)
- the *plucking method* (manual or by machine)
- the *processing* of the tea leaf (drying, fermenting, mixing) to form a wide variety of types.

The British perfected tea cultivation in their colonies in India and Ceylon in the 19th century, to such an extent that the quality designations and sorting grades they developed were recognized all over the world and are the ones still used today.

Subdividing the qualities into these traditional sorting grades is only possible to its full extent where plucking is done manually. For business reasons, modern plantations are unfortunately increasingly using machinery for plucking nowadays. Modern countries such as Malaysia have practically no manual plucking any more.

In Japan, machine plucking and selection has been developed to such an extent that no loss of quality ensues. Analyses of good Japanese green teas confirms this. Only the most expensive types of tea and frequently the first harvest of spring (first flush) are plucked manually.

In China and Japan, as well as for practically all kinds of green tea, quality categories are used less and then only to a limited degree.

The basis for naming the wide variety of *qualities* is formed by the following designations:

BROKEN
Cut-up tea, mostly done in a 'cutter'.

FANNINGS
Second-finest, second-smallest sifting; never whole leaves or whole shoots.

FLOWERY
High-quality tea with young leaf buds.

FLUSH
New shoot. An entire small leaf with bud is considered to be top quality; 'one bud and one leaf' with leaves of a standard size if possible and a pure aroma.

FIRST FLUSH
First sprouting in the spring.

SECOND FLUSH
Second sprouting after the interim-monsoon period (rainy season).

AUTUMNAL FLUSH
Autumn sprouting after the major monsoon rain.

Between these sprouting phases, plucking breaks are made by cutting back the tea shrubs. If plucking is continued during the rainy season, the harvest is called 'rain tea'.

ORANGE
This refers to the Dutch royal dynasty of Orange and means a royal tea, i.e. a tea of the highest quality.

PEKOE
This refers to the 'white' pecco blossom, its leaf tips and the young shoots which are still white underneath when picked. Botanically, the pecco blossom is not a blossom, but the youngest bud on a tea plant which is still covered with white down.

TIP / TIPPY
Leaf tips; the proportion of young bud leaves (tips) is correspondingly high.

The following examples are abbreviations for the designation of *leaf grades* and *sortings*:

OP
Orange Pekoe (elongated, whole leaf)

FOP
Flowery Orange Pekoe (as above, but with some bud content)

TGFOP
Tippy Golden Flowery Orange Pekoe (thin, whole leaf with high bud content)

BOP
Broken Orange Pekoe (main type of 'Broken tea')

FBOP
Flowery Broken Orange Pekoe (cut-up tea with some bud content)

OF
Orange Fannings (second smallest sorting, mostly for teabags).

*The author at a tea producer's in Darjeeling (India). Every day
the harvest is tested as ready-to-drink tea.*

In spite of great respect for the extremely valuable tea plant, I have the feeling that, with so many alternatives in quality and sorting designations, this is more of a cult which leads to confusion. In addition, these designations are practically limited to Britain's former colonies and thus to black tea only.

Of course, there is nothing wrong with a sensible subdivision of qualities, but the factors that appear more important to me are tea with as little residue as possible, taste, its origins in terms of climate and soil properties, perfect processing, size of leaf and contents or active ingredients. By 'lack of residue' I mean the lowest possible proportion of heavy metals, insecticides or fertilizers or, even better, none at all!

Of course, manual plucking and the corresponding manual and detailed care in processing, results in a high-quality tea which, after siftings, can be more easily allocated to the various grades than is possible with machine plucking.

The two production methods are as follows:

Orthodox

is the traditional processing by hand; this also includes manual plucking by women.

CTC

stands for 'crushing, tearing, curling'. This highly streamlined method of production mostly includes machine plucking. A modern and much more economical style of processing, this does not permit any categorisation of leaf tea, but produces 'broken' and 'fannings' qualities. The frequently mentioned loss of taste caused by this process is disputed by modern technology specialists. In particular, it appears that, with careful machine plucking and processing, the active ingredient content of the tea is maintained in the best possible way. By far the major part of world production uses the CTC method today.

A Small Dictionary of Tea

AFTERNOON TEA

This is not a type of tea, but a traditional British afternoon light meal with tea to drink and often small sandwiches and scones to eat (a typical British light plain cake, q.v. recipe on page 83).

ASSAM GREEN TEA

Please refer to the chapter on 'Green Tea'.

ASSAM TEA

Tea (black tea) from *Camellia assamica*, mostly, but not always, originating from Assam (eastern India). Tea producers in Darjeeling also cultivate Assam tea.

BANCHA

See the chapter on 'Green Tea'.

BLACK TEA

General term for all fermented teas. Please refer to the chapter on 'Black Tea'.

BLEND/BLENDED TEA

Tea blends which are often skilfully put together from a variety of sources, mostly a speciality of traditional British tea-houses and tea producers.

BREAD AND BUTTER TEA

See under 'Rain Tea'.

BRICK TEA

A traditional way of storing and trading tea in China, Tibet and Mongolia. The dried leaves are ground in a mortar, mixed with rice water and then pressed into special brick shapes. 'Bricks' of this type are mostly decorated with ornamentation and names (q.v. illustration, page 21).

CREAM TEA

This is not a type of tea, but a traditional British afternoon tea with scones, clotted cream and jam.

DARJEELING

The most famous of the tea cultivation regions in north-east India. Tea grows here in the uplands at altitudes between 1,000 and 2,400 metres above sea-level. Darjeeling is known for the production of high-quality, 'flowery' tea, mostly black tea. For some years now, green tea has again been increasingly produced in Darjeeling.

DUST

The smallest particles of ground tea, mostly for teabags.

EARL GREY

Black tea with the added flavour of

pure bergamot oil (oil from a citrus fruit/primitive orange).

ENGLISH BLEND

Mostly a mixture of tea from the original British colonial areas of Darjeeling, Assam and Sri Lanka (Ceylon).

GARDEN TEA

Garden tea is one of which the origins are known, i.e. the tea garden (plantation) is precisely known and designated. This can signify an additional quality designation.

GENMAICHA

This is Bancha tea with the addition of toasted, natural rice grains.

GREEN TEA

General term for unfermented and non-oxidized tea, i.e. all green teas. This book is mainly dedicated to this type of tea. Only green tea still contains all the active ingredients; these have made it a popular drink and also a fascinating natural remedy.

GUN POWDER

See the chapter on 'Green Tea'.

GYOKURO

See the chapter on 'Green Tea'.

HIGH TEA

This is not a tea quality, but traditional tea-drinking in honour of the British royal family. Every afternoon, between four and five o'clock, high tea, as it is called, is served at Buckingham Palace. The traditional small sandwiches and scones are also part of this.

Traditional hotels in Australia, India and even Singapore still serve high tea.

In Britain, the tradition, i.e. the meaning of 'high tea', changed decades ago. Nowadays, 'high tea' refers to an early evening meal (cf. 'afternoon tea' and 'cream tea').

HONJICHA

See the chapter on 'Green Tea'.

ICED TEA

Iced tea is simply tea with ice, served cold as a thirst-quencher. Iced tea first received a mention at the World Exposition in St. Louis in 1904. A young salesman, Richard Blechynden, reputedly had the idea of pouring hot tea into a glass of ice cubes instead of serving the usual ice-cold drinks. His iced tea became a huge success.

Today, iced tea is available as instant tea in the form of herbal mixtures of all kinds, and with additives in a wide variety of flavours; it generally has nothing to do with the original iced tea. Commercially available iced tea provides no guarantee of quality for the tea used. Good iced tea is best prepared at home (q.v. recipes on pages 70 and 72).

INSTANT TEA

Instantly soluble powdered tea, manufactured by various drying and extraction processes, making up approximately 40% of the U.S. tea market. Flavour and quality never live up to the expectations of tea fans.

JASMINE TEA

Genuine jasmine tea is semi-fermented Chinese tea with the addition of real jasmine blossom. Beware of tea with added jasmine flavourings!

Being semi-fermented, jasmine tea is thus an acceptable alternative to green tea since it is frequently available in restaurants, while green tea mostly is not.

KEEMUN

A first-class, extremely carefully processed black tea from Keemun in China (Anhui province).

LAPSANG SOUCHONG

Large-leaved black tea with a smoky taste from China, also called 'smoked tea', produced by 'roasting' over a fire of resinous wood or frequently flavoured only artificially.

MATE

Yerba mate – a stimulating beverage. Mate tea does not come from a type of *Camellia* but from a type of holly (*Ilex paraguariensis*) in South America. It is thus neither black tea nor green tea. However, mate tea is wrongly sold by some dealers as green tea. Mate tea has only one thing in common with green and black tea, and that is that all three contain caffeine.

MATTCHA

See the chapter on 'Green Tea'.

MONGRA

See the chapter on 'Green Tea'.

OOLONG

Semi-fermented tea from China or Taiwan (Formosa).

RAIN TEA

Also called 'Bread and Butter Tea'. This is the tea harvested during the rainy season and mostly of low quality.

SCENTED TEA

General term for flavoured teas. Made with qualitatively inferior kinds of black tea to which are added genuine essential oils: man-made oils identical to those occurring in nature or, still in many countries, the health-wise highly problematical fruit esters.

Genuine tea connoisseurs have nothing but disdain for all these teas even when flavoured 'naturally', since the high concentration of flavouring agents is a danger to health.

SENCHA

See the chapter on 'Green Tea'.

SPICED TEA

Spiced tea is black tea to which mostly tropical spices such as cinnamon, ginger, cardamom, star anise, allspice, cloves, vanilla, etc. have been added. These teas are popular in Europe, particularly during the winter. They offer no guarantee of good quality and are frequently additionally flavoured with essential oils.

TEABAGS

In 1904, the New York tea dealer Thomas Sullivan is said to have sent his customers tea samples in small silk bags. He had probably invented the first teabags.

Now, around 70%–80% of all tea (black tea and less frequently, green tea) worldwide is distributed and used in teabags. Teabag quality has undoubtedly been greatly improved, although it still varies enormously. Teabags thus tend to be more of a concession to convenience, e.g. at the workplace or when travelling. Modern teabags even have double chambers and the best, most neutral material is non-woven. Teabag qualities rarely fulfil the highest expectations where flavour and selection are concerned.

THÉ À LA MENTHE

Speciality and traditional beverage of the Arabs, Berbers and Bedouins of North Africa. This type of tea is green tea combined with the fresh leaves of Arabian mint and prepared with a lot of sugar. Beware of tea flavoured with peppermint!

THEA VIRIDIS

See the chapter 'Green Tea'.

WHITE TEA

A rarity, originally from Kwangsi, China. Very fine, mild tea; the young, still downy buds are only air-dried.

YERBA MATE

See under 'Mate tea'.

The Regency Restaurant & Tearooms

26-28 The Pantiles, Tunbridge Wells, Kent TN2 5TN Telephone: 0892 525353

See our board for delicious home-made specials

— SPECIALITY TEAS —

Pot per person:

Traditional English, Darjeeling, Earl Grey, Assam, China,
Lapsang Souchong, Rose Pouchong, Ceylon 95p
Pure Camomile, Pure Peppermint, Mixed Fruit, Rosehip & Hibiscus,
Fennel & Lemon Balm, Camomile & Spearmint 95p
Lemon 90p

The tea of connoisseurs for almost 300 years

— TRADITIONAL ENGLISH TEAS —

Served all day

Cream Tea – Two Home Baked Scones, Cream and Jam, Pot of Tea
£3.20 per person

Afternoon Tea – Round of Sandwiches,
Two Scones with Cream and Jam, Pot of Tea
£5.25 per person

High Tea – Plaice and Chips, *or* Lemon Sole Goujons and Chips,
Bread and Butter, Ice cream, Pot of Tea
£5.50 per person (Goujons 20p extra)

— HOME MADE CAKES & DESSERTS —

The Active Ingredients
in the Tea Leaf

The main active ingredients in the tea leaf are caffeine (formerly called theine), tannin (flavonols), theophylline, theobromine, fat, wax, saponins, essential oils, catechins, carotene, a lot of vitamin C, as well as vitamins A, B_1, B_2, B_{12} and P, fluoride, iron, magnesium, calcium, strontium, copper, nickel and zinc, trace elements such as molybdenum and phosphorus, as well as over 300 additional substances, some of which are aromatic. The quantitative proportions of these active ingredients vary according to the area of cultivation (altitude, climatic region) and the growth stage of the leaf. Younger leaves and buds have the greatest caffeine content. Older leaves have correspondingly larger amounts of tannin.

Like all dried plant elements used in naturopathy, tea is designated a drug in medical terminology. The word 'drug' comes from Low German and means 'dry' and 'drying'. (It is thus not used to refer to 'hard drugs' or addictive drugs.) A business dealing in these was called a 'Drogerey' and later 'Drogerie' in German.

The ingredients of all plant-based drugs should not be considered or dismissed as monosubstances, despite the most advanced and sophisticated methods of analysis. Isolated monosubstances basically have an entirely different effect from the combinations of active ingredients found in nature. Plants and different parts (leaves, blossoms, roots, etc.) have grown harmoniously with all their natural components and must therefore be assessed holistically. It is the sum of all the ingredients in a plant that is responsible for its effects on the human organism.

Careful drying usually prevents any changes to the active ingredients. This is a natural form of conservation which we have learned from nature itself. A typical example of this is dried seeds which, when stored well, will still be capable of germinating after many years.

In contrast, fermentation and oxidation which occur when black tea is processed are biochemical and chemical processes which bring about the corresponding changes in the active ingredients of a drug. This explains the major differences in effect and taste between black tea and green tea.

The Stimulating Effect of Black Tea and Green Tea

Irrespective of the type of tea, there are some complicated connections between the various factors which affect the greater or lesser stimulating effect of tea. These factors include the growth stage of the leaf, the brewing time and naturally the amount of tea used.

The stimulating effect of tea is caused by the alkaloid caffeine which is linked with the tannin in the tea leaf. Since caffeine dissolves well in hot water, almost the entire quantity of caffeine is dissolved in the infusion within the first 1–2 minutes, without the tannin. The result of a short brewing time is thus a drink with a high level of caffeine that is no longer linked to the tannin and which is rapidly absorbed when the tea is consumed. Caffeine also has a stimulating effect on the central nervous system and brain functions.

If left to brew for longer, i.e. around 4–8 minutes, the tannin and many other active ingredients in tea start to dissolve gradually. Tannin has the effect of partially preventing or delaying the caffeine being absorbed in the stomach and intestines. Although this longer infusion time causes a stronger taste, the caffeine effect is weaker or delayed. Experience has proved that this delayed effect can stretch the cumulative effect of caffeine to 10–12 hours with frequent, daily tea-drinking. Sensitive people can have their sleep affected late at night by an overdose of afternoon tea (by black tea, in particular).

It is a fact that longer brewing (4–8 minutes) can definitely never have a calming effect since tea leaves simply do not contain any ingredients that could be considered calming, and these could not be created by longer brewing. So the 'soothing' claims on tea packaging are false and improper and, in the case of black and green tea, absolutely false and misleading. The terms 'highly stimulating' (short brewing time) or 'slightly stimulating' (longer brewing time) would be correct and meaningful.

The caffeine quantity can be reduced by pouring a little boiling water over the amount of tea to be used and then sieving this off after half a minute. Afterwards, the tea is prepared as usual.

The most digestible tea is achieved by using a small amount (max. one level teaspoon per cup) of tea leaves and longer brewing time (4–6 minutes) – naturally without the addition of sugar or artificial sweeteners. Tea left to brew for a short time, however, has a milder taste.

When not consumed to excess, tea has a stimulating, but not irritating, effect. In contrast to earlier assumptions, this stimulating effect does not raise blood pressure (q.v. 'The Curative Effects of Green Tea'). Excess intake of caffeine, however, can cause an increase in blood pressure.

Caffeine – Addictive Drug or Medicine?

For more than a century, caffeine was the best-known active ingredient that could be isolated and analyzed in tea, coffee beans and other plant drugs.

As already mentioned, tea contains several hundred active ingredients that have been identified in the meantime. These include catechins, in particular epigallocatechin (q.v. 'Research into Green Tea', page 54), and others which play a much greater role in the healthful effects of tea than caffeine. Caffeine can only base its special role on the fact that it has been talked about for years, and its stimulating effects have been studied.

The term 'theine', as the caffeine in tea was called for a long time, is no longer used since it is chemically identical to caffeine and only differs in its combination with various other ingredients (q.v. 'Tea and Coffee Compared', page 41).

Caffeine as a monosubstance

From a chemical aspect, caffeine belongs to the xanthine derivatives found in various plants with the exact designation 1,3,7-trimethyl xanthine. With similar chemical formulas, the two alkaloids theophylline and theobromine are also present in small quantities in the same plants in which caffeine is found.

Caffeine was isolated as a monosubstance by a chemist in 1820. Goethe is said to have given this chemist several coffee beans with the instruction to analyze them and study the effects on people and animals. As a result of this early isolation of pure caffeine, this ingredient was considered to be the primary active ingredient in tea and coffee.

Research results on this have been continually expanded for decades.

Caffeine-containing plants around the world (besides the tea plant)

Cocoa (cacao), botanical name: *Theobroma cacao (Sterculiaceae)*

The cacao tree is native to Central America and is cultivated in many tropical countries. Cocoa is obtained from the seeds (cocoa beans) which contain 0.05–0.4% caffeine. Fresh cocoa beans are fermented with their pulp (the fruit pulp surrounding the seed) and then husked. The cocoa butter is separated from the cocoa mass by melting.

Guarana, botanical name: *Paullinia cupana (Sapindaceae)*

This tree is native to Brazil and is cultivated in Central America to some degree. The seeds of this tree are used to make a paste containing 4–8% caffeine, which is then used as an ingredient in stimulating drinks.

Coffee, botanical name: *Coffea arabica (Rubiaceae)*

The coffee tree is native to East Africa, mainly Ethiopia, and is cultivated worldwide in tropical areas. The seeds (coffee beans) contain 0.7–2.6% caffeine when raw and 1.3–2.9% caffeine when roasted.

Cola, cola nut, botanical name: *Cola nitida (Sterculiaceae)*

The cola tree originates from tropical Africa. The seeds (cola nuts) contain 1.5–3.5% caffeine.

Mate, botanical name: *Ilex paraguariensis (Aquifoliaceae)*

Mate, a type of holly, is native to sub-tropical South America. The leaves contain 0.3–1.5% caffeine.

What the above-named plants all have in common is that they contain caffeine in various combinations and that they are all grown in the tropics. However, they also thrive, like the tea plant and the mate tree, in sub-tropical regions. All these trees have been used from time immemorial by the local populations as a source of pleasure and good health. Thanks to these examples it was possible gradually to refine luxuries from these drugs – such as chocolate from cocoa, luxury teas from tea and mate leaves, stimulating drinks from the cola nut and coffee, and also to use some of them as remedies.

Products containing caffeine

Besides being found in tea, coffee and in stimulating drinks such as cola beverages and those containing guarana, caffeine is also contained in some pharmaceutical preparations used to treat migraine, headache and rheumatic ailments. Caffeine not processed as a monosubstance but as an extract of the cola nut or coffee is highly popular in homeopathy for sleep disturbances or sedation purposes.

A more recent analysis shows the comparison of caffeine content in various beverages produced in normal portions:

Beverage	100 ml/1 dl	Caffeine
Fuji green tea, biological cultivation	contains	46 mg
Gun Powder green tea	contains	36 mg
Bancha tea	contains	13 mg
Darjeeling black tea	contains	45 mg
Mate tea	mate infusion contains	18 mg
Coffee/normal coffee	dependent on the method of preparation and the type of coffee contains	66–98 mg
Espresso	dependent on the espresso machine and the type of coffee contains	177–354 mg
Cocoa drink	contains	7 mg
Cola drink	cola beverage contain	9 mg

The average caffeine content calculated in the amounts normally used in Western countries:

1 teacup	170 ml/1.7 dl	Fuji green tea	78 mg
1 teacup	170 ml/1.7 dl	Gun Powder green tea	61 mg
1 teacup	170 ml/1.7 dl	Bancha tea	22 mg
1 teacup	170 ml/1.7 dl	Darjeeling black tea	77 mg
1 teacup	170 ml/1.7 dl	Mate tea	31 mg
1 coffee cup	150 ml/1.5 dl	Normal coffee	123 mg
1 espresso cup	50 ml/0.5 dl	Espresso	133 mg
1 coffee cup	150 ml/1.5 dl	Cocoa	11 mg
1 bottle	300 ml/3.0 dl	Cocoa drink	21 mg
1 bottle	300 ml/3.0 dl	Cola beverage	27 mg

For these calculations, consideration was given to the fact that 85% of most of the total caffeine content of the raw product dissolved in the beverage during the preparation of the tea and coffee.

From this summary of caffeine analyses, readers can calculate their daily caffeine consumption. A study of this type is particularly interesting in calculating children's caffeine intake, which should also include the stimulants which contain guarana (I prefer not to describe these as 'beverages').

Further study of this book will reveal how the caffeine in coffee or tea can have different effects.

The effect of caffeine

In standard doses of 50–200 mg, caffeine mainly affects the cerebral cortex. This alleviates tiredness of any type. In greater doses, the vasomotor and respiratory centre is stimulated. The fact that this does not cause any increase in blood pressure is because the coronary blood vessels and those in the skin and kidneys are simultaneously dilated.

High blood pressure results only from an excessive consumption of high caffeine dosages. An excessive dosage causes restlessness, racing thoughts or even heart rhythm disturbances. Actual poisoning with caffeine or preparations containing caffeine is very rare. However, medical circles have calculated that a lethal dose of caffeine for humans is around 10g. *In order to kill yourself with caffeine, you would have to drink approximately 80 cups of coffee or around 140 cups of tea within a very short space of time – which borders on the near-impossible.*

During pregnancy, a frequently-repeated overdose of caffeine, i.e. more than 600 mg per day, can have an abortive effect. However, this quantity of caffeine corresponds to a daily consumption of at least fourteen cups of tea with the highest caffeine content possible.

For most people, caffeine in the relevant beverages has a weaker effect at sea-level than when the same quantity is consumed at an altitude of 1,000 meters, when the effect is noticeably stronger.

After drinking coffee, the effects of caffeine appear relatively quickly, with the maximum effect approximately 30 minutes afterwards, which then gradually declines within the next 2–3 hours. After drinking tea, the effects are delayed even with the same amount of caffeine, but the effect lasts longer (q.v. chapter 'Tea and Coffee Compared', page 41).

The effects of caffeine from tea and coffee

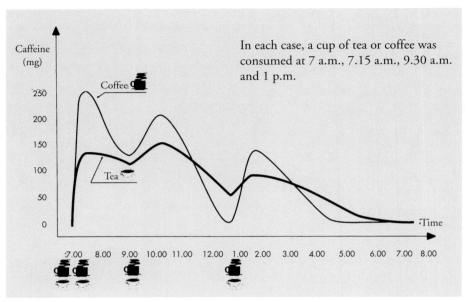

This proves that the effect of caffeine can only be precisely determined as an isolated monosubstance. If caffeine is contained in the parts of a plant, it has very differing effects because of its connection with tannin, chlorogenic acid, etc. and the presence of many other active ingredients. This phenomenon can be observed from the differing effects of black and green tea. Naturopathy teaches that it is not the active ingredients as monosubstances that trigger off the overall effect but the sum of all the active ingredients which have been harmoniously put together by nature.

The effect of caffeine in coffee, tea, etc. is increased firstly by the natural content of the active ingredients theophylline and theobromine which are similar to caffeine and, secondly, by the synergy, as it is known, of caffeine with alcohol. In tea with rum, or coffee with schnapps, the admixture of alcohol has a synergetic effect, i.e. it strengthens the caffeine in these beverages.

After oral intake, by drinking tea or coffee, the caffeine is quickly absorbed from coffee and more slowly from tea, but in both cases almost completely. The resultant waste products in the urine are di- and monomethylxanthine, monomethyl uric acid, etc.

Caffeine allergies

Allergies of this type tend to be rare, but do exist. An allergic reaction to caffeine after consuming coffee, tea or even chocolate is manifest in a more or less strong itching that generally affects the whole body for some time (1–3 hours).

Interestingly, tests on allergic people have revealed that these people had absolutely no allergic reaction after drinking green tea! I have to explain this phenomenon by stating that caffeine triggers off allergies only in fermented, oxidized or roasted products such as black tea or coffee. These processing methods, as with the manufacture of cocoa and chocolate, cause caffeine to make new combinations, which is not the case with green tea. Probably caffeine allergies are actually allergies to the different caffeine combinations and not to pure caffeine itself.

Is caffeine addictive?

Even a regular daily dose of caffeine in natural products causes no lasting damage. Some people, however, frequently react to overdoses with sleeplessness, inner unrest, etc. In contrast, caffeine can promote sleep for older persons, which probably has to do with improved circulation to the brain and increased cardiac activity.

Addiction is a condition which can be caused by the repeated use of drugs (abuse of narcotics, medication, alcohol, nicotine). Addiction is marked by a mental and/or physical compulsion to continue consumption of the causative substance and continually to increase the dosage. Milder types of addiction, without these critical features, manifest themselves in physical indisposition when the drug is discontinued, or in mental dependence.

For many people, drinking coffee or tea is actually a habit which does not involve continually increasing the amount consumed. In addition, and particularly in connection with the regular drinking of green tea, it is a proven fact that in many countries this habit clearly causes no damage to the body or the mind.

Getting used to a stimulating effect is still going in the direction of dependence, however. It is a fact that even when this habit is discontinued for days or weeks there are never any withdrawal symptoms, as experienced by real addicts or real types of addiction. Let the experts argue and the tea-drinkers decide at what point the daily quantities change from being a habit to dependence, and when addiction begins.

Would you like to test whether you are a tea- or coffee-addict? It's very simple. Starting on a predetermined day, drink neither tea nor coffee for two weeks and note how it affects your reactions and bodily functions. Breaks of this kind in order to test yourself can have value.

What can we learn from these findings?

If the dangers are known, it is easier to deal with them rationally. Paracelsus, the Swiss physician and alchemist, taught us *that nothing or everything is poisonous* and all that matters is the dosage. The following advice is thus valid:

- Infants should never be given beverages containing caffeine. With tea, as already mentioned, there is the possibility of heavily reducing the caffeine content by means of special preparation or changing to tea low in caffeine (Bancha).
- When preparing tea, the correct amount should be observed; in any case, tea-drinking at bedtime should be correspondingly limited.
- Tea, in a somewhat different way from coffee, increases mental powers, which many people find pleasant. With an overdose of beverages containing caffeine, there is a danger of an overactive brain conflicting with physical tiredness. On a continuous basis, this can lead to a dangerous imbalance.
- Tea and other beverages containing caffeine cannot replace sleep.

Tea and Coffee Compared

The enjoyment of caffeine in the form of tea is very different from that of coffee. As already mentioned, caffeine is combined with tannin in a fresh tea leaf, while caffeine in coffee is combined with chlorogenic acid. Together with the other characteristics of these beverages, this plays an important role in health-giving effects.

Tea does not increase the fatty acid content of the blood. Coffee, however, causes a substantial increase in the fatty acid proportion in the blood by preventing the breakdown of fatty acids. Tea, in particular *green tea*, even has an anti-arteriosclerotic effect. Nor does tea contain any residue from roasting.

In different ways, both beverages can cause sleep disturbance. The caffeine combination in coffee has a stimulating effect on the heart and circulation, while that in tea affects the central nervous system. Once again, green tea has a milder effect than black tea. Generally speaking, black tea *(but not green tea)* has a more or less aggressive effect on the stomach and nervous system.

Unlike coffee, tea – in particular green tea – is an alkaline beverage which counteracts superacidity.

The various *black teas*, like coffee, are drunk purely for *pleasure*, while *green tea* is drunk for both *pleasure and health*. Nevertheless, black tea is more digestible than coffee and *green tea is additionally a remedy of inestimable value*.

The effect (resorption) of caffeine from coffee is generally considerably faster than is the case with tea. Thus the caffeine in coffee has a shorter effect than after drinking tea. The fast effect of caffeine is like drinking espresso standing up at a counter, in contrast to less hectic tea-drinking in pleasant surroundings and in pleasant company. In today's world, deliberate tea-drinking during a moment of peace and quiet is the ideal answer to combating stress and promoting mental activity.

Black Tea

Black tea is produced by fermenting the leaf, which is slightly pre-dried with warm air, wilted and broken or curled under the influence of heat. When broken, the cell contents come to the unprotected surface of the leaf. From a chemical point of view, this is only partially a fermentation that is made possible by the leaf's enzymes; it is simultaneously an oxidation for which the correspondingly prepared leaves are placed for 20–40 minutes in a special oven set at a temperature of between 35°C and 80°C. During this process, tea oil develops which is composed of polyphenols and other degradation products. This process also reduces the tannin content by around 10%. The polyphenols which develop are responsible for the orange-brown colour of tea and of course for the brown teeth of passionate black tea drinkers. The caffeine content barely changes during fermentation and oxidation, but does become rather more effective as it is released partially from the tannin.

However, during the black tea production process, the valuable health-giving epigallo catechins are altered and important other ingredients, including vitamin C, are destroyed. The holistic and major health-giving properties are lost. A high-quality natural product is thus turned into just a beverage.

Black tea as a beverage

Despite these 'negative' aspects of black tea, I would like to say a few words in favour of genuine, pure black tea. If tea connoisseurs do not expect any healthful benefits from their tea, but appreciate black tea as a beverage with various pure qualities, then the existence of this beverage is justified. It is up to you or tea connoisseurs to treat this beverage properly and be aware of the differences from green tea.

Depending on where it is grown (climate, etc.), the plucking stage of the leaves and the length of the fermentation and oxidation processes, various tastes are produced in black tea. However, this has nothing to do with the artificial flavourings of some types of tea using fruit esters (synthetic flavourings), essential oils, etc. Tea connoisseurs disapprove of these *scented teas* (e.g. mango, apple, blackberry and other artificially flavoured types of black tea). These are no longer genuine teas, but *fake* teas.

Green Tea

As a result of this fermentation and oxidation, many of the components beneficial for our health (catechins, vitamins, etc.) are changed or destroyed in the production of black tea. *None of these processes are used in the production of green tea.*

Depending on the quality or country of origin, the leaves used in green tea are harvested and air-dried. The most usual method is steaming, as it is known, in which the freshly-plucked leaves are briefly treated with steam and then dried. This short steaming process eliminates the danger of fermentation. Other methods even include 'roasting' the dried leaves.

The leaves for green tea are also plucked at different stages and in different seasons, which again affects their caffeine content, the proportions of the many ingredients to each other and the taste.

The best-known and scientifically-proven curative properties of tea identified in practical trials *only* apply to *green tea*.

'Brewing philosophies' for green tea vary according to country and tradition, from using boiling or boiled water, or water only warmed to 80°C, as well as between shorter or longer brewing times. Pouring off the first infusion (as already mentioned) reduces the caffeine content and the slightly 'bitter' taste.

Green Tea and its Processing

1　TEA FIELDS
From the end of April onwards, the tea is plucked by hand and the leaves are taken immediately to the processing plant.

2　STEAMING
The tea leaves enter the steamer via a conveyor belt and are then cooled.

3　CURLING
The machine curls and dries the tea leaves.

4　SPINNING AND DRYING

5　RE-CURLING AND DRYING
Second and last curling of the leaves. The final stage is drying.

6　READY FOR SALE
The tea leaves are now ready for sale.

Additional processes

7　SPECIAL PROCESSING
Aim: other leaf shapes e.g. by cutting the tea leaves.

8　FINAL DRYING OR ROASTING
For special types of tea
Aim: a different taste.

9　BLENDING PROCESS
Rare with green tea: the mixing of different sorts.

10　PACKAGING

11　TRANSPORT

12　COMMERCIAL TRADE

This machine for 'curling' tea has been in operation in Darjeeling (India) for over one hundred years.

State-of-the-art, electronically-controlled machines for the processing of green tea in Nagoya (Japan).

The best-known commercial varieties of green tea are as follows:

THEA VIRIDIS
Green tea with no designation of origin, no quality guarantee and originating mostly in China, Taiwan (Formosa), Sri Lanka or Indonesia. The designation 'Thea viridis' was formerly used as the term for parent tea plants, mostly of Indonesian origin.

CHINA
GUN POWDER
Typical Chinese green tea. The leaves are steamed for a short time and then curled to pellet-shaped balls during the drying process.
JASMINE TEA
Genuine jasmine tea is also a Chinese speciality. This is semi-fermented tea (fermentation is halted at a certain point by steaming) and real jasmine blossom is added. Strictly speaking, jasmine tea should not be called green tea.

INDIA
ASSAM GREEN TEA
A quality similar to the above, but from the plantations in Assam. However, most of the Assam teas are black teas with only a small proportion of green tea being produced, which must be designated as such.
Darjeeling also produces Assam Green Tea from the *Camellia assamica* plant.
DARJEELING GREEN TEA
is a green tea quality (Mongra, etc.) from Darjeeling, processed according to the usual method by brief steaming, etc.

JAPAN
Traditionally, Japan produces only green tea. The best qualities are mostly designated by the names of the plantations, etc. Japan produces the largest selection of top-quality green teas.
SENCHA
Sencha is the type mostly consumed in Japan. The plucked leaves are quickly taken for processing, steamed for approximately 30 seconds and then shaken in hot air and dried until, after being curled several times, they resemble green needles. Sencha tea is available in various qualities dependent on the

harvesting stage of the leaves. Sencha tea is slightly bitter in taste. The tea itself is a light gold colour.

GYOKURO

The name means 'noble dewdrops'. Processing is similar to that of Sencha. The main difference is in the leaves, which grow 90% in the shade. In addition, only the most delicate and softest leaves are used. This special tea is considered to be the absolute best and most expensive sort. It has a strong taste and is less bitter than Sencha. Connoisseurs prepare this tea with boiled water that has been allowed to cool to 50°C to 60°C. The tea is gold-green in colour.

MATTCHA

Mattcha is the most expensive of the tea qualities; one of its uses is for the tea ceremonies. Like Gyokuro, its leaves thrive in the shade and are processed similarly. This dried tea is ground to a fine powder in a stone mill shortly before sale or use. To make tea, the green tea powder is placed in a tea dish with water cooled to 60°C and then stirred with a small bamboo brush until the powder has dissolved. Foam forms on the surface with the typical taste. This highly stimulating tea is deep green in colour.

BANCHA

Bancha tea is considered the 'lowest' sort of tea. Processing is similar to that of Sencha tea, but the leaves are only harvested at the end of the season. For this reason, they are thicker and more fibrous and contain less caffeine than the other sorts.

Bancha tea is frequently described as 'three-year tea', probably because leaves up to three years old are harvested. This tea is mentioned and recommended particularly in connection with a macrobiotic diet.

HONJICHA

This is generally a roasted Bancha tea; it is brownish in appearance and bitter in taste. The caffeine content of Honjicha is correspondingly low.

The Best-Known Green Tea Qualities

1

2

3

4

5

6

7

8

9

CHINA
1   GUN POWDER
2   JASMINE TEA

INDIA
3   ASSAM GREEN TEA
4   DARJEELING GREEN TEA

JAPAN
5   SENCHA
6   GYOKURO
7   MATTCHA
8   BANCHA
9   HONJICHA

The Curative Effects of Green Tea

Dutch doctor Nicolas Diveks (1593–1674) paid a tribute to tea in his book *Die Arznei* with the following words:

'Nothing surpasses tea. Drinking tea keeps people free of all possible illnesses and promotes a long life. Tea gives energy, and is very helpful for those who study or work late into the night. It is quite right to drink 12 cups of tea every day.' This praise for tea can be complemented by many similar quotes from the old Chinese and Japanese cultures.

Since the 17th century, researchers, doctors and naturopaths have repeatedly turned their attention to tea and to green tea in particular. According to a wide range of recent research results that we will be examining in the next chapter, the following curative effects can all be ascribed to green tea:

- relieves stomach and intestinal problems
- reduces blood cholesterol levels
- strengthens the blood vessels
- favourably influences the heart and circulation
- prevents and heals arteriosclerosis
- has anti-inflammatory effects
- has a favourable influence on normalizing thyroid functions
- promotes blood circulation and skin regeneration
- in particular, increases mental performance and, to a certain extent, physical performance
- combats depressive moods
- promotes the healing of liver illnesses
- combats rheumatism if taken over a longer period of time
- counteracts the formation of kidney and gall stones
- prevents tooth decay as a result of its ideal fluoride content
- according to the latest findings of a Japanese research team headed by Dr Hirota Fujiki, has a proven prophylactic effect against the risk of cancer
- has a diuretic, detoxifying effect
- is effective as an antioxidant
- is an excellent source of iron, fluoride, important trace elements and vitamins

The ancient and revered cultures of China and India claimed to know a form of light energy and named this 'Chi'. It was the belief that this energy was present in a wide variety of natural elements as a healing energy. Modern physics is also investigating these fine particles, which have been christened 'biophotons'. This energy, radiated by cells, may also be partially responsible for the healing properties of the active ingredients in medicinal herbs. It is an additional benefit of green tea that these 'light cells' remain 'undamaged', in contrast to black tea.

There are thus many reasons to turn to the centuries-old art of tea-drinking – to green tea. If we substitute it for coffee and black tea, we are drinking an equally 'stimulating' but much more meaningful beverage, both in terms of health and pleasure.

Scientific Studies on Green Tea

Before we take a comprehensive look at the most modern and wide-ranging study of green tea conducted by Dr Hirota Fujiki, I have listed some of the most significant findings of the past in abbreviated form:

- Igor Dolov published a summary of studies conducted by various former Soviet Russian institutes (Physiological Institute in Kiev, Biochemical Institute of the Scientific Academy in Moscow):

  Green tea promotes healing in cases of radiation damage. Tests on animals and clinical trials on humans indicate curative effects in cases of chronic hepatitis, nephritis and dysentery.

- In 1976, the Medical College in Calcutta published an extensive study: green tea lowers cholesterol levels and protects against the onset of heart attacks.

- Okyama University, Japan, Prof Takuo Okada:

  Green tea is 20 times more effective than vitamin E in preventing the formation of superoxide – a free radical.

- Kagoshima University, Japan, Dr Ichiro Mori:

  Green tea contains ideal natural combinations of zinc and copper. Pregnant women, in particular, need a lot of zinc. Since this mineral is one of the most important trace elements that a woman's body needs at this time, green tea is the ideal drink during pregnancy.

- University of Tokyo, Japan, Department of Medicine and Dentistry, Prof Dr Masao Onishi:

  One cup of green tea a day would be sufficient to reduce tooth decay in schoolchildren by half. Even just rinsing the mouth with green tea after meals is an effective way of preventing tooth decay. The natural fluoride in green tea is highly effective. Additional antibacterial compounds are also effective against the tooth decay bacterium, streptococcus mutans.

- Tohoku University, Japan, Dr Meuro; Japanese Academy of Medicine, Dr Fukui; Nagoya University, Japan, Dr Aoki:

  Green tea contains an enzyme that affects the triggering mechanism of high blood pressure. Green tea helps in cholesterol transformation and thus prevents arteriosclerosis. Dr Aoki even maintains that, if green tea is consumed on a regular basis, it helps protect against strokes as well as various cardiac problems and illness caused by ageing.

- Hamamatsu University Shizuoko, Japan, Dr Eiichi Hayashi:

  After many years of study and experiments, Dr Hayashi was able to prove that the tannin compounds contained in green tea form a chemical compound with strontium-90. Drinking green tea tannin thus prevents the absorption of strontium-90, which is released, for example, as fallout in atomic power station accidents, by up to 30%, since this amount will be disposed of by the body, together with the tannin in green tea.

Research into Green Tea

Alongside the empirically well-known and scientifically-confirmed various curative effects of green tea, comprehensive studies have determined that green tea also has an anti-carcinogenic and antioxidant effect.

A Japanese doctor of medicine, *Dr Hirota Fujiki*, was for many years on the staff of the Max-Planck Institute and is today the director of the Saitama Cancer Research Institute in Japan. The institute does basic and clinical cancer research. It is supported by the Saitama Prefecture and, depending on the research topic, it receives additional support from the Japanese Ministry of Culture or Ministry of Health. With his express permission, I will give an abbreviated version of his research report.

Background

In Japan, the studies were conducted on the basis of well-known conditions and facts.

- The tea plant *(Camellia sinensis)* was officially imported to Japan from China in the 12th century and green tea exclusively was produced. Tea-drinking and tea cultivation spread amazingly quickly and, today, the daily consumption of green tea is a part of Japanese culture. The Japanese drink tea practically throughout the day.

- Statistically, life expectancy in Japan is 82 years for women and 76 years for men, which, on a worldwide basis, is the highest anywhere (1995 figures).

- In the Japanese prefecture of Shizuoka, the largest tea-growing area, there is the lowest incidence of deaths from cancer in the whole of Japan. Cancer of the stomach is practically unknown in this region.

These facts gave many Japanese researchers the idea of linking all these findings with the regular drinking of green tea. Intensive efforts were therefore made to find the relevant effects and ingredients in green tea.

The work of Dr Fujiki and colleagues

In 1985, a team headed by Dr Fujiki started research into cancer-retarding or cancer-curing substances in general.

During the course of these studies, which were financed and supported by the Japanese Ministry of Health as well as other organizations and foundations, the team of researchers succeeded in isolating probably the most effective anticarcinogenic substance in green tea, Epigallocatechingallate (EGCG).

EGCG

Following many initial trials conducted on mice in which a wide variety of cancer tumour promoters were applied to the skin or carcinogenic substances were introduced, the clear result was that EGCG:

- retarded the tumour promoters on the skin and
- prevented carcinogenesis in the digestive tract and various organs. It also healed existing tumours in the intestines.

These comprehensive trials with mice also revealed the working mechanism of EGCG. In clinical trials, it was later proved that the anticarcinogenic effect of EGCG was also valid in the case of humans:

- EGCG retards the development of metastases in the lung.
- EGCG retards the growth of cell carcinomas in the lungs, stomach, intestine, liver and the skin.
- EGCG also reduces the toxic effect of smoking.

According to Dr Fujiki, clinical trials for cancer of the breast, pancreas and prostate have not yet been concluded.

Dr Fujiki's conclusions

We are convinced that green tea, taken on a daily basis, with the main active ingredient EGCG in combination with other active ingredients in green tea, can be an ideal and cheap means of preventing cancer. The old and widespread belief held in many Asian countries that green tea taken on a regular basis is a beverage with high healthful value and many curative effects has been confirmed. Alongside its anticarcinogenic effect, it also has a beneficial effect on the heart, circulation, liver, diabetes and cholesterol levels.

How can green tea be sensibly used?

On the basis of his research findings, Dr Fujiki recommends drinking a cup of green tea ten times a day. This roughly corresponds to one gram of EGCG. *It should be noted that a Japanese teacup contains a maximum of 1 dl (100 ml) and the corresponding amount would be around 6 to 7 European (Western) teacups.*

The tea should be measured sparingly; the maximum amount is one level teaspoon of dry tea per cup. Dependent on the reaction of the tea drinkers, the effect of the caffeine should also be taken into consideration; the corresponding amount of tea should thus be consumed in the morning and around midday rather than in the evening. Naturally, the changeover from old habits to green tea means that there is hardly any 'capacity' left for enjoying coffee.

Dr Hirota Fujiki answers some questions

What tips can you give people in Europe who are interested in changing over from coffee or black tea, for example, to green tea?

Dr Hirota Fujiki: It is generally not easy to change one's lifestyle, and old habits of drinking coffee or black tea. Since black tea originates from the same plant as green tea, many people may find it hard to believe that green tea is supposed to have so many advantages over black tea. If people take a serious look at the subject and study the scientific publications, then the changeover will be easier. We have repeatedly found that these people soon learn to appreciate the taste of green tea. For non-tea-drinkers, we will be producing green tea tablets in the near future.

You are the director of the Saitama Cancer Research Institute. In addition to drinking green tea, can you give us any further health-promoting advice in terms of lifestyle or nutrition?

Dr Hirota Fujiki: American scientists recently published the results of a new study: out of 90 substances presumed to have an anticarcinogenic effect, 8 reacted effectively in the tests. These were some vitamins and trace elements that are present in natural food. This also confirms what we have long been recommending – that natural health food is of enormous importance in cancer prophylaxis, as well as for the health of heart, circulation, liver, etc. in general.

I very much appreciate your efforts in making our research findings known to the Swiss population and the rest of Europe. Cancer prevention is one of our main tasks and is extremely important for every individual.

Dr Hirota Fujiki at the 'Saitama Cancer Research Institute' in Japan.

Some suitable storage containers for tea.

How to Store Tea

In contrast to medicinal herb drugs which generally have a 5%–10% residual moisture content, tea is almost completely dried as a result of the typical processing method. This means that it can be stored in closed, airtight containers, bags, etc. without causing any mould to form. Properly stored, tea will keep its taste over a longer period of time.

For transportation from the plantation – where processing mostly takes place – to its destination, plywood chests are traditionally used, each containing 10–25 kg. A more modern, perhaps even better form of packaging, is in smaller vacuum-sealed bags with a capacity of 1–5 kg.

Packaging is of major importance, not just for transport to the dealers, but also to retailers and consumers. Only top-quality storage guarantees that the quality expected can be maintained for months or even years.

- Tea must always be stored well-sealed and in a dry place. Tea caddies made of wood, special tin or porcelain with well-fitting lids are ideal. Packets of tea that are coated and opaque are also suitable. All containers, however, may only be used for tea, to prevent any contamination of its taste.

- Tea should be stored in a cool, dark place, i.e. away from light, sunlight or heat.

- Keep tea packaged in small quantities. When measuring out tea, dampness (e.g. steam) can damage the tea.

- Perfectly stored tea can be kept for up to five years with practically no loss of quality. Green tea loses its taste less quickly than black tea.

The Correct Way to Prepare and Drink Tea

Tea-drinking should be a source of pleasure and enjoyment, even if green tea is taken only as 'medicine'. The taste, contents and amount should be perfect. Only when it is prepared correctly and carefully does it meet these requirements.

In China and Japan, the appropriate tea ceremony is part of the old tradition of tea-drinking, ranging from the simpler preparation rituals in secular circles to the meditative, devoted tea ceremony of Zen Buddhism. Geishas (traditional Japanese women servants) also played an important role in secular tea ceremonies.

During colonial times, India's tea culture was heavily influenced by the British, with a great deal of sugar and milk still being added to tea in India and Britain to this day. The tea in these examples, however, is mostly black tea.

The amount of time and effort you expend on tea preparation is for you to decide. In any case, however, it is worth knowing the background to 'perfect' preparation.

The basic principles and the utensils for this are the *teapot*, the *teacup* (both together make up the *tea service*, as it is known), *water*, the choice of *type of tea* and the *amount*.

The teapot

The most suitable materials are porcelain, pottery and glass. Cast iron is also suitable, but should have an enamelled interior. In order not to ruin the taste of the tea, a teapot should really only be used for tea and never for coffee. A teapot should only ever be rinsed out with hot water (never use washing up liquid or rinsing agents) and then left to air-dry.

Traditional teapots and the attractive and functionally perfect 'bodum' glass pots are ideal for tea preparation.

The teacup

The best material is porcelain, and for special occasions fine bone china. Fine pottery cups can also be used. The fine, delicate tea taste of good-quality green tea suits a fine, lightweight and rather small teacup which holds a maximum of one decilitre (100 ml).

Some teacup volume comparisons:
–   Large Western teacup in heavy porcelain: contents 1.7–2.0 dl / 170 ml–200 ml
–   Cups in special Western tea services in finest bone china: contents 1.3–1.5 dl / 130 ml–150 ml
–   Japanese and Chinese teacups in finest bone china: contents 0.8–1.2 dl / 80 ml–120 ml

Chinese porcelain has been famous for centuries. The Portuguese and the Dutch first put precious Chinese tea porcelain on the European market when they imported tea into Europe. The original teacups in Europe also had no handles, which is still the case in Japan and China today.

The water

Water quality is of major importance for a good cup of tea. Ideally, this should be springwater that is not too hard. Water should be taken from the cold tap and always boiled; never use water from an immersion heater. If the water is chlorinated and/or fluoridated, it requires filtering first.

Green tea is not brewed with boiling water, since this makes the tea too bitter. The boiled water should be left to cool for a moment first.

The type of tea

There is also a wide variety of tastes among the various types and qualities of green tea. Try out several good quality teas and make your choice. Drink different ones at different times as appropriate and perhaps serve a top-quality, expensive tea only on special occasions.

If your preferred choice of tea is based on a fondness for the country of origin of these wonderful leaves, then you are forgiven!

The amount

The correct amount is probably the most important aspect of a good cup of tea. Mostly, it is overdone. As with medicinal herbs, a large quantity never means a superior effect. Too high a dosage of a herbal infusion can have the opposite effect to what was intended – a highly-dosed green tea has an unpleasant taste and the caffeine content is much too high! When the tea is too strong, it tastes bitter and unpleasant and there is every possibility that a 'tea beginner' is put off for life! The following basic principle in naturopathy is also valid for a good green tea:

Small quantity is always right,
large quantity is always wrong!

A freshly-brewed green tea is much paler, more delicate in colour, ranging from golden-green to golden-yellow; black tea is mostly brown to dark brown. Do not let yourself be tempted to use a larger amount because of green tea's weak colour.

The correct amount, therefore, does not mean pouring randomly out of the packet and into the teapot, but requires a teaspoon as a measure for best results. The ideal amount is 2 g tea per cup: this corresponds to a *level* teaspoon. A heaped teaspoon contains as much as 5 g, which is far too much.

Sugar?

The question mark actually says it all! Genuine tea connoisseurs drink tea, and green tea in particular, unsweetened to avoid impairing its taste and healthy effect. In its countries of origin – China, Japan and wherever it is nurtured as a tradition – green tea has always been consumed unsweetened.

Drinking tea with milk and sugar developed in the British tea culture and always in connection with black tea. Fortunately, this habit is also gradually changing in Britain with growing health awareness.

The need to sweeten tea is frequently caused by using too much tea: trying to correct the bitter or even repulsive taste. When the correct amount and the correct method of preparation are used, tea never requires its taste correcting with sugar or artificial sweeteners. We are all aware of the damage done by industrial sugar to our health. In addition, green tea without sugar and milk is a healthy, calorie-free beverage.

The tea ball

A tea ball, whatever its type, is *not* a suitable tea-making utensil. Dried tea in a tea ball swells during preparation and closes the pores of the tea ball almost completely from the inside. This prevents the interchange between the solvent water and the ingredients of the tea. The tea ball is useless for both herbal infusions and for good tea!

The tea sieve

The tea sieve, as it is called, has a 'tea part' of sieve-like mesh which provides a better opportunity for extracting active ingredients from the tea. Not the ideal method, but acceptable, e.g. for restaurants.

Sieve inserts

For the preparation of just one cup of tea, the tea inserts available commercially are suitable for holding the corresponding amount of tea. Bamboo sieves look nice and natural, but alter the taste of the tea.

The Classic Way of Preparing Tea

After this introduction to the basic facts, we can now take a look at the *classic method of preparing* a normal quality green tea, e.g. Sencha, Gun Powder, etc.:

1. **WARM THE TEAPOT AND CUPS**
Depending on the time of year, and particularly in winter, the teapot and the cups should first be filled with hot water.

2. **AMOUNT**
2 g tea (1 level teaspoon) per cup is put into the empty teapot. For around 4–5 cups and more, the rule is: 1 level teaspoon per cup and one for the pot.

3. **POUR HOT WATER OVER THE TEA**
The boiled, but no longer boiling water (leave it to stand for a moment after boiling) is poured over the tea in the teapot.

4. **EMPTY THE PREVIOUSLY WARMED CUPS**
While the tea is brewing, there is time to empty the cups filled with hot water.

5. **POUR THE TEA INTO THE CUPS**
Leave the tea to brew for the required time. Short brewing times (2–3 minutes) produce a highly stimulating tea that is milder in taste; longer brewing times (4–6 minutes) result in a stronger, slightly bitter taste. The stimulating effect is slightly weaker, but of longer duration (q.v. 'The Stimulating Effect of Black Tea and Green Tea', page 32). First of all, just a small amount of tea is poured into each cup, then each is filled in turn until all are full or there is no more tea in the teapot. This method ensures equal quality and strength for each cup of tea.

The tea leaves in the teapot can be brewed a second time. Since the leaves have already absorbed some water, the brewing time can be reduced by at least half of the first brewing time.

*The preparation of 'Mattcha tea' is a special and meaningful
ritual both in Zen Buddhism and secular circles.*

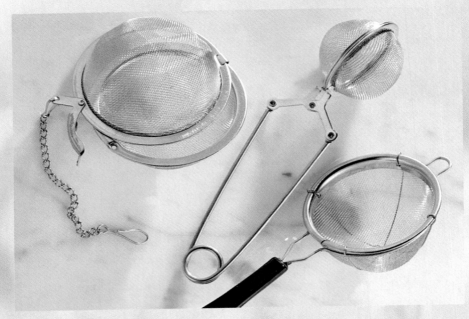

*Tea sieves and sieve inserts are more suitable for tea preparation
than a tea ball.*

The 'Mattcha tea' is first pulverized in a stone mortar, then placed in a cup using the 'CHA-SHAKU' bamboo spoon and water is poured over it. The 'CHASEN', an artistic bamboo whisk, is used to stir until the tea powder has dissolved. An exclusive tea for special occasions!

Connoisseurs use water cooled to 50°C–60°C after boiling to brew particularly high-quality, exclusive Japanese teas such as 'Gyokuro' or 'Mattcha'. The tea is then allowed to brew for 2–2½ minutes and the amount used is frequently slightly higher than usual.

If you want to keep tea warm for a longer period of time, the taste keeps better in a Thermos jug than on a hotplate. If tea is kept warm for longer than 15–30 minutes on a hotplate, the taste slowly changes.

Teabags

A cup of green tea can also be made with a good-quality teabag in accordance with the method given. It would be wrong and a pity not to pay the same attention to teabag tea.

Electric teamakers

In recent times, electric teamakers have appeared on the market and, to some extent, have disappeared again. This is the reason that no brand names are mentioned here, which does not necessarily mean that these machines are bad. They are mainly suitable for the quick and easy preparation of breakfast tea. If more time is available, however, it is worthwhile preparing tea in the usual way.

Preparation in brief

The abbreviated instructions below summarize the aspects of 'classic' preparation that you can choose to include in your preparation, as you wish.

Preparation:
- Pour boiled water over the dry tea leaves, *one level teaspoon per cup.* (Precise measurement produces the finest taste.)
- A short brewing time (2–3 mins.) produces a highly stimulating tea with a mild taste; longer brewing times (4–6 mins.) result in a stronger taste and slightly less stimulating effect.
- Caffeine content is greatly reduced by pouring a little boiling water over the tea leaves and straining it off after 30 seconds. Then prepare the tea as usual.

A Selection of Tea Recipes

The following recipes are limited to those which are really worthwhile additional uses for green tea as well as a few traditional 'teatime treats' and exclusive 'tea desserts'.

You probably expect to find some herbal tea mixtures. However, in naturopathy, there are some medicinal drugs that are so broad in spectrum and act so holistically that they should not be used in mixtures. Among these drugs we find the ginseng root and, in particular, green tea. Green tea is thus the main ingredient in our recipes, with the selected ingredients, as with careful seasoning, increasing or emphasizing the desired effect.

Green Tea on the Rocks

- Freshly-brewed green tea
- Ice cubes

1. Fill a glass with ice cubes

2. Sieve the freshly-brewed green tea and pour into the glasses.

TIP: it couldn't be simpler – healthy and calorie-free

Family Iced Tea

for 1 litre of tea

- 1 litre water
- 5–6 level teaspoons green tea or Bancha tea (less stimulating)
- ½ cinnamon stick
- 1–2 teaspoons honey
- 1 teaspoon lemon juice
- Several dashes of Angostura bitters

1. Prepare by pouring water over the green tea or Bancha tea as required with the addition of the crumbled cinnamon stick. Allow to brew and then sieve the tea.

2. While the tea is still warm, stir in the honey, lemon juice and Angostura bitters. Place the tea in the refrigerator to chill.

3. Serve the iced tea decorated with peppermint or balm leaf.

PRODUCT DETAIL:
Angostura bitters, a root and spice extract from Venezuela, has been sold for over 100 years.

Green Tea for the Sporty

for 1 litre of tea

- 1 litre water
- 5–6 level teaspoons green tea or Bancha tea
- 1–2 teaspoons honey
- A few drops of lemon juice

1. Prepare by pouring water over the green tea or Bancha tea as required. Allow to brew and then sieve the tea.

2. While the tea is still warm, stir in the honey and lemon juice.

3. For a warm drink, pour the tea into a Thermos flask; for a cold drink into a water bottle.

TIP: Green tea is a revitalizing thirst-quencher. When half of the contents have been consumed, fill up with fresh water. In this way, the still-tasty tea can be diluted at will, without you having to take too much liquid with you.

Spiced Tea

Tea mixture

- 100g jasmine tea (semi-fermented tea) or Bancha tea (green tea low in caffeine)
- 3–4 cm cinnamon stick
- 2 clove heads
- 2–3 cm vanilla pod, finely chopped
- Honey
- Angostura bitters

1. Crush cinnamon stick, cloves and vanilla pieces in a mortar. Mix with the jasmine or Bancha tea leaves. This mixture will store well for several months.

2. For 1 litre of tea, use 5 to 6 level teaspoons of the mixture and pour on 1 litre of water. Allow it to brew and then pour through a sieve.

3. Flavour each cup of tea with a minute amount of honey and 2 to 3 dashes of Angostura bitters.

TIP: This makes a superb beverage with a 'Christmassy' taste for cold winter evenings.

Tea with Rum

for 1 litre of tea

- 1 litre water
- 5–6 level teaspoons green tea or Bancha tea
- White rum
- Honey
- Angostura bitters

1. Pour water over green tea or Bancha tea, as preferred. Allow to brew and then sieve the tea.

2. Flavour each cup of tea with 1 teaspoon of rum, a minute amount of honey and a few dashes of Angostura bitters to taste.

Green Iced Tea Coupe

for 1 litre of tea

- 1 litre water
- 5–6 level teaspoons green tea
- 1–2 teaspoons honey
- Juice of ¼ lemon
- 4 scoops vanilla ice cream
- Whipping cream
- Grated rind of 1 unwaxed lemon

1. Pour the water over the green tea. Allow to brew and then sieve the tea.

2. While the tea is still warm, stir in the honey and lemon juice. Chill.

3. Place the vanilla ice cream in tall tea glasses. Pour over the cold tea. Garnish with a generous blob of whipped cream and lemon rind. Serve with a drinking straw.

Scones

makes approx. 14 scones

- 1½ cups milk (approx. 200 ml / 2 dl)
- 20 g butter
- 400 g wholemeal flour
- 1 pinch sea salt
- 2 teaspoons baking powder

1. Preheat oven to 160°C.

2. Warm milk and butter.

3. Mix flour, salt and baking powder together. Stir in the warm milk and form into a dough.

4. Divide the dough into two. From each portion shape scones 4–5 cm in diameter or cut rounds with a pastry cutter. Set the scones on a greased baking tray and bake them in the pre-heated oven for 15 to 20 minutes.

VARIATIONS:

Add to the dough: raisins (2 tablespoons), crisp cooked pumpkin (100 g), powdered vanilla (2 pinches), ground cinnamon (2 teaspoons), acacia honey (1 teaspoon), dried pears or dried apricots (2 tablespoons).

Green Tea Pastries

- 360 g spelt flour or wholemeal flour
- 3 teaspoons baking powder
- 1 teaspoon salt
- 50 g soft brown sugar
- 50 g butter, softened
- 2 free-range eggs
- 100 ml / 1 dl strong green tea
  (made with approx. 3 g green tea leaves)
- 10 g Demerera sugar for sprinkling over

1. Preheat oven to 180°C.

2. Mix flour, baking powder, salt and soft brown sugar (50 g) together. Rub the butter into the flour until the mix resembles breadcrumbs. Beat the eggs with the green tea and add. Knead to a smooth dough.

3. Roll out the dough on a floured surface to a thickness of 1 cm. Cut 5 cm squares. Fold each square into a triangle but do not flatten.

4. Place the pastry triangles on a greased baking tray. Brush with green tea and sprinkle with Demerera sugar.

5. Place the triangles in a preheated oven and bake for around 25 minutes. Serve warm.

Green Tea Parfait

serves 5

- 150 ml / 1.5 dl water
- 150 g soft brown sugar
- Grated rind of ½ an unwaxed lemon and ½ an unwaxed orange
- 50 ml / 0.5 dl green tea (made with approx. 5 g green tea leaves)
- 3 free-range eggs
- 300 g / 3 dl whipping cream
- Additional whipping cream for decoration

1. Boil water, sugar and grated lemon and orange rind. Allow to stand for 5 minutes. Pass through a sieve and keep the syrup.

2. Mix the sugar syrup and green tea. Add the eggs. Whisk with a balloon whisk in a hot bain-marie (80°C) until a creamy mass forms. Whip the cream until cold over cold water (add some ice cubes).

3. Carefully fold the whipped cream into the cooled cream. Do this gently to prevent the mass from collapsing.

4. Transfer the parfait mass to a freezer container or single portion containers and freeze for 5 to 6 hours.

5. To serve, turn out into a dish or divide up into portions and decorate with the whipped cream.

TIP: Serve with prune purée, fruit preserved in rum or with a syrup of boiled figs.

Green Tea for Children?

If green tea did not have a stimulating effect, but only its recognized health benefits, there would be no question about it. The stimulating effect of caffeine, however, requires caution in the case of children and, in particular, for infants. Besides green tea, there are also beverages such as iced tea, etc. which may also contain caffeine and should also be investigated as to their suitability as a drink for children.

Without their parents' awareness, many children consume caffeine – often at a very early age. This is mostly contained in chocolate, beverages containing cocoa, cola drinks, etc. in small quantities (q.v. pages 35 and 36). Whether stimulating or not, these products of our civilization are not promoters of good health.

Depending on country and family habits, children are often given coffee – mostly made with all milk – at too early an age. The health aspect should be given greater consideration, particularly since the addition of milk neither makes the coffee healthier nor more digestible.

However, there is still the question of tea. Green tea definitely does not belong in a baby's bottle and is even less suitable as a thirst-quencher in the large, uncontrolled quantities that are always available for somewhat older children.

In Japan, children learn to drink green tea relatively early on in life and, in Tibet, the traditional tea is mixed with yak butter when given to children. However, it should be remembered that in that country there is a lack of the beverages and products containing hidden caffeine.

There is no generally valid rule for deciding from what age onwards, before or after puberty, a young person should drink green tea. Once again, the quantity and the time of day for drinking the tea are important. Consideration should be given to the question of whether the problematical drinks mentioned can be replaced by green tea.

For children, herbal teas are primarily the most suitable thirst-quenchers for consumption in large quantities, e.g. peppermint, lime-blossom, balm, verbena, etc., or the corresponding blends. A good alternative to normal green tea and as a change from herbal teas is Bancha tea (q.v. page 47), which is suitable as a cold summer drink. For health reasons, whether you have herbal tea or Bancha tea, these should not be sweetened with sugar but possibly with a very small amount of honey.

In the case of teenagers, green tea can noticeably improve mental agility, e.g. even for examinations, when consumed in sensible quantities.

Green Tea and Sport

The content and the effects of green tea speak for themselves – there is no drink for athletes that is more ideal or more natural. Green tea can also be consumed cold as a revitalizing thirst-quencher.

Increased mental agility results in greater concentration, motivation and stamina – even for longer-term activities such as golf, hiking or mountaineering. Physical performance is also increased as a result of the ideal combination of the active ingredients, the high proportion of vitamin C, other vitamins, trace elements, etc. Green tea stimulates but does not agitate!

Depending on the quantity consumed, the tea can be diluted a little. To harmonize with blood sugar levels during sports, green tea can be sweetened with a small amount of honey.

The addition of a few drops of lemon juice to this sports drink makes it even more refreshing as a thirst-quencher. This 'sport green tea' is 'purely natural'. You need not have any worries about preservatives, food colourings or synthetic vitamins. Nature has created everything in harmony and, moreover, this tea can be made in any quantity and within a short space of time.

Green Tea during Pregnancy

During pregnancy, it is particularly important for women to enjoy good health and receive the necessary trace elements. This is the reason why vitamin and iron preparations are frequently prescribed during pregnancy. It is evident from the studies in the comparisons between coffee and green tea that coffee impairs or even prevents the absorption of iron and other trace elements. On the other hand, green tea, besides its many other benefits, is an excellent source of iron and zinc. Both these elements are of tremendous importance during pregnancy.

Together with a healthy diet, it is obvious that the changeover from coffee and tea to green tea is to be recommended and, if possible, that drinking coffee should be stopped before becoming pregnant. Giving up old habits is often easier before, rather than during, pregnancy. Green tea also promotes a good mood and vitality.

Pregnant women sometimes react with greater sensitivity to the caffeine in the tea. To avoid sleeping difficulties during pregnancy, a time when the body is subject to major transformation, it is recommended that the following, previously-mentioned facts be noted for green tea in late afternoon and evening:

- Caffeine content is effectively reduced if a little boiling water is poured over the dry tea leaves and then sieved off after 30 seconds.
- After sieving, prepare the tea as usual.

Bancha tea (q.v. chapter on Green Tea, page 43) contains significantly less caffeine, but still retains all the active ingredients and trace elements important for health. It is thus highly suitable as a thirst-quencher, particularly during pregnancy.

Green Tea during the Menopause

The change of life or menopause with its reduction in hormone production is part of every woman's life and is as nature intended. These years can and should mean a transition to a new and positive stage in life. Nevertheless, many women, often as a result of their lifestyles, experience it as a time of increased emotional sensitivity, restlessness, etc.

These feelings and their physical condition lead many women to increased coffee consumption, which largely prevents the absorption of trace elements such as iron and calcium and does not improve the state of the nervous system. It is precisely at this time of change that it is extremely important to provide the body with the necessary vitamins and trace elements.

Green tea and Bancha tea, which is slightly lower in caffeine content, contain active ingredients that are absolutely vital for the organism at this time.

The switch from coffee or black tea to green tea or the special type, Bancha, is once again the ideal contribution to improved health. The stimulating and uplifting emotional effect is also very welcome during the menopause.

A study conducted by Professor Takuo Okada of Okayama University in Japan reports that the ideal combination of active ingredients in green tea complement or even exceed those of vitamin E. This mainly affects the reduction of superoxide formation in the body, which also slows down the ageing process.

Undoubtedly, green tea cannot be considered a wonder cure for every type of menopausal problem. However, within the framework of a healthy lifestyle, and healthy nutrition in particular, green tea offers a highly recommendable supplement for greater well-being during these years. The daily enjoyment of green tea in sensible quantities can help to reduce the number of vitamins, mineral preparations or even medication taken at this time.

Green Tea and Diets

The question of whether green tea can be or is compatible with diets is one that requires a few introductory remarks.

Diets are modern, but not everything that is modern is valuable and good. The wildly confusing range of countless nutritional methods is joined by around 20–30 new diets every season. A diet is always incomplete, never holistic, but mostly one-sided and aimed at a particular target, such as slimness or for the benefit of a particular organ. Anyone living according to the dictates of nature has no need of a diet. This means natural health food, which takes into account the activities and the lifestyle of the person concerned. I do not consider sensible food combination, as well as a vegetarian style of nutrition, as diets. The only worthwhile diet would be fasting, as the most effective way of elimination of waste and detoxification in the body and spirit. *Correct fasting* is thus a precondition, therefore.

Green tea can be ideally combined with all your eating habits. The same is true if you decide to go on a temporary diet or, for whatever reason, are put on one. The trace element and vitamin content of green tea is an ideal supplement in either case, as well as providing all the healthful benefits already mentioned.

When fasting, it is beneficial to change to a special green tea, Bancha tea, since this contains three times less caffeine than other types of green tea (q.v. Bancha tea, page 47).

In the interests of good health, it is extremely important that *absolutely no* coffee or black tea is consumed while fasting!

Green tea, the healthy way to drink tea.

Some Requests

After this closer look at the tea plant and the secrets of green tea, I would like to point out that these marvellous properties and curative effects of the tea leaf refer only to *green tea*. When tea is processed to make black tea, most of these properties are lost, the active ingredients are destroyed or altered and black tea is reduced to just a normal beverage.

If you have learned to appreciate the special, natural taste of green tea by means of correct preparation and a good choice and have, perhaps, also experienced the unique effects, you will no longer miss black tea.

We are living at a time when civilization's illnesses such as rheumatic problems, arthritis, allergies, tooth decay, gum problems, skin problems, depression, a wide range of metabolic disorders, cancer, symptoms of deficiency and many more are still on the increase. If we compare these disorders with the possible health-promoting effects of green tea, it would appear that this medicinal plant, which has been acclaimed for thousands of years, is particularly right for our present time.

The effect of every natural remedy should be supported by a healthy lifestyle and corresponding natural health food. The same is true for green tea. Perhaps in one way or another, readers will take time to examine their previous lifestyles and nutritional habits as a result of drinking green tea.

I would like to conclude my report on green tea with a few requests:
- that more and more people will consider the original form of tea-drinking – and green tea in particular
- that consumers will be more critical, i.e. better informed, when buying tea so that teas with so-called 'nature-identical' aromas or scented with fruit esters which cause health problems will disappear from the market
- that the tea culture is revived and nurtured in European cafés, tearooms and restaurants of all categories. This presupposes a wide selection of teas and green teas, loose tea if possible, served accordingly and with good teabags for individual cups

- that during training for the catering professions, knowledge of tea as a product is correspondingly developed.

Many people, perhaps without thinking, often say: 'I only drink tea when I'm ill.' Perhaps this book will help to change this attitude. This also means being able to differentiate between green tea, black tea and the herbal infusions, as they are known, for medicinal purposes or enjoyment. Everything at the right time and for the right occasion. Medicinal herbs and tea complement each other!

Perhaps, with your new-found knowledge, you can help some of these requests to come true.

GREEN TEA – THE BEVERAGE FOR BODY, MIND AND SPIRIT!

Words of Thanks

While writing this book, I needed important information and data.

I would like to express my special thanks to Dr Hirota Fujiki for his cooperation and for providing me with his team's research results from the 'Saitama Cancer Institute', Japan.

My thanks are also due to K. Tanaka (Japan) for his specialist information, Richard Schmid (Cantonal Laboratory, Lucerne) for conducting the caffeine test, Werner Speck for the drawings, Hans Schwarz for the charts, Dr Stefan Schindler for his assistance in providing medical data, Ingrid Schindler for journalistic appraisal, Anne-Marie Gisler for the word-processing of the manuscript, graphic designer Ursula Mötteli for her sensitive design of the book, as well as my wife, Hanny, and son, Thomas, for putting together and producing the recipes.

About the Author

Peter Oppliger, born 1940; certified Swiss pharmacist, trained naturopath, homoeopath and phytotherapist. Studied in nutrition at the East-West Foundation in Boston, USA.

Seminar leader for autogenics and yoga teacher (trained at the Himachal-Pradesh University in India).

The author is the owner of a drugstore in Lucerne, Switzerland. He organizes and conducts nature and naturopathy study trips in Switzerland and overseas. He organizes courses in naturopathy and conducts health weeks and medicinal herb excursions. Various teaching appointments. Founder of the historic drugstore and the medicinal herb garden at the Swiss Open-Air Museum of Rural Life in Ballenberg, Switzerland, where he is also in charge of naturopathy exhibits.

Bibliography

Hans G. Adrian, Rolf L. Temming,
Arend Vollers
Das Teebuch
Verlag C. J. Bucher,
Munich / Lucerne

Wilhelm Baumüller
Aleijos T'U CH'UAN
Grüne Wunderdroge Tee
Braumüller-Verlag, Vienna

Peter Martin Urtel
Die Kunst TEE zu trinken
BLV Verlagsgesellschaft,
Munich Vienna, Zurich

John Blofeld
The Chinese art of TEA
George Allen, London

John Blofeld
Das TAO des Teetrinkens
Diedrichs-Verlag, Munich

Lesley Mackley
Tea & Coffee
Salamander Books Ltd, London

Schaffner, Häfelfinger, Ernst
Pharmaka Kompendium
Arboris-Verlag, Hinterkappelen

Publications by the Tea Promoters
Calcutta, India

Publications by the Saitama Cancer
Center Research Institute, Japan

Publications by Japanese tea producers

Wichtl
Teedrogen
Wissenschaftliche Verlagsgesellschaft,
Stuttgart

Katalyse-Umweltgruppe, Cologne
Chemie in Lebensmitteln
Zweitausendeins, Frankfurt

Hoppe
Drogenkunde
Walter de Gruyter, Berlin

Mutschler
Arzneimittel-Wirkungen
Wissenschaftliche Verlagsgesellschaft,
Stuttgart

Schneebeli-Graf
Blütenland China
Chinesische Nutz- und Heilpflanzen
Birkhäuser, Basle

Gesundheits-Brockhaus
Brockhaus F. A. GmbH, Leipzig

Römp
Lebensmittelchemie
Thieme-Verlag, Stuttgart

Forth, Heuschler, Rummel
Pharmakologie und Toxikologie
Spektrum Akademischer Verlag,
Heidelberg

Index